The —
LITTLE BOOK OF
PSYCHOLOGY

Emily Ralls & Caroline Riggs

summersdale

THE LITTLE BOOK OF PSYCHOLOGY

An Hachette UK Company
www.hachette.co.uk

Summersdale Publishers Ltd
Part of Octopus Publishing Group Limited
Carmelite House
50 Victoria Embankment
LONDON
EC4Y 0DZ
UK

www.summersdale.com

Printed and bound in Poland

ISBN: 978-1-78685-807-8

CONTENTS

WE ARE A WAY FOR THE COSMOS TO KNOW ITSELF.

CARL SAGAN

Introduction

The human brain is the only living thing that can study itself. Perhaps that is the reason you picked up this book? Not only can the brain study itself, it is also capable of doing so while processing an incredible amount of information from your surroundings.

For example, while you are reading this page your brain is receiving information as electrical signals from your eyes. It is instantly recognizing where it has seen these lines and shapes before, recalling that they represent letters and words, and linking them to the meanings it has paired them with in the past.

At the same time, your brain may *not* have drawn your attention to the sounds that are around you. It is constantly filtering out tones that may not be an immediate danger to you. It has already decided that it is safe for you to ignore these sounds, but would instantly alert you if a sabre-toothed tiger walked into the room.

Perhaps you are not currently aware that your hypothalamus, in the middle of your brain, has received signals from your skin and monitored the temperature of the environment that you are in. It has made adjustments to keep your vital organs at a constant temperature.

It could be that you are now slowly becoming more distracted from these words as we point out that you are blinking without much consideration, and that you have stopped noticing which parts of your body are touching the chair you may be sitting in, or how your feet are resting on the floor. Your brain was taking care of all of this, while trying to learn about itself.

A hundred billion neurons are taking care of you, while simultaneously *being* you.

These biological processes in the brain that contribute to our day-to-day experiences and behaviour can be observed, measured and manipulated using a variety of modern scientific techniques. These days, we can observe the brain as it processes information in real time by using brain scanning techniques such as functional magnetic resonance imaging (fMRI), but this was not always the case, and the biological study of the brain itself represents only one element in the study of psychology. While we now understand that the brain may be said to "contain" the mind, there are many facets of human experience that cannot be observed using biological techniques and require more subtle, and more subjective, reasoning to attempt to understand them.

Throughout this book we will discuss various attempts in the history of psychology to explain our behaviours, from the more traditionally scientific approaches, such as biological and behavioural psychology, to the more subjective approach of Freud and psychodynamic psychology.

The History of Psychology

It's difficult to know where to begin when describing the history of psychology. In part this is due to the difficulty in separating the study of psychology from that of philosophy. In ancient Greece, philosophers discussed subjects that we would commonly associate with psychology today, such as the soul, the mind and the nature of thought. However, it wasn't until around the 1800s that psychology emerged as a discipline in its own right, when German scientist **Wilhelm Wundt** (1832–1920) began using "the scientific method" to study human behaviour.

Wundt's 1874 book, *Principles of Physiological Psychology,* was a first major attempt to link the studies of physiology (how our organs and organ systems function) and human behaviour. He opened the first official Institute for Experimental Psychology in Leipzig, Germany in 1879 and pioneered the use of introspection as a research method.

Try introspection

Light a candle and watch it flicker, play a single note on an instrument or smell a flower. Now say out loud how this makes you feel, or what thoughts you have. This is introspection: examining your own mental processes.

Wundt's method of introspection was innovative because he was attempting to study the thought processes themselves, rather than observable behaviour or the structure of the brain in isolation. Participants were guided to examine and report their own internal thoughts and to self-observe. Trained staff would monitor the experience, presenting planned sensory stimuli in a controlled way, such as sounding a metronome or turning on a light. Wundt recognized the importance of using experimental methods to study human behaviour, and emphasized the need to be able to repeat an experiment within the same conditions, so that the reliability of results could be tested.

Since then, the scientific study of human behaviour has flourished, with psychologists employing the scientific method with varying degrees of rigour to explain how the interaction between our biology and our experiences can shape our behaviour.

In this book we will discuss the major fields of study in psychology today, from Freud's psychodynamic approach, which emerged in the early twentieth century, to modern brain imaging techniques.

The Biological Approach

Where our thoughts and behaviours originate from has been a source of much reflection by philosophers and scientists during human history, and is still not a question with an absolute answer. However, as our understanding of biology improves, so does our understanding of psychology. In this chapter, we will explore the anatomy of the brain, the influence of genetics and how our evolutionary past may have influenced human behaviour.

It was around 2,500 years ago that Hippocrates first argued that it was the brain that was responsible for human thought and consciousness, and not the heart, as Aristotle believed. During the centuries that followed, many theories were put forward about how the brain may contribute to the human experience, including the Greek philosopher and surgeon Galen's ideas (developed in the second century CE, but still popular even as late as the seventeenth century) that the brain acted almost like a pump, pushing fluid through nerves to our organs. If it wasn't for scientists' morbid experiments attempting to re-animate executed prisoners in the nineteenth century, we may never have considered that our bodies were actually controlled by electrical signals travelling to and from our brains. At a time when electricity was not yet widely used, this was an important development in our knowledge of biology.

However, it didn't matter how inspired scientists were by the idea of an electrically charged biological supercomputer controlling our bodies; they unfortunately lacked the medical knowledge to keep a willing patient alive long enough to open up their skull and actually observe anything. In a time before brain imaging technology, such as Magnetic Resonance Imaging (MRI) and Positron Emission Tomography (PET) scanners, our information came from the misfortunes of people who had endured horrendous injuries and survived, allowing scientists to observe the changes to their personality, behaviour or memory as a result.

The most famous of these case studies took place in 1848 when Phineas Gage, an American railway construction foreman, suffered a brain injury when a 43-inch-long iron pole was propelled through his skull during a workplace accident. Gage was using the pole to tamp explosives into a hole during the construction of a railroad bed in

Vermont. The pole pierced Gage's frontal lobe but miraculously did not kill him. It did, however, leave him with impaired cognitive functions and personality changes. Gage's doctor (Dr John Harlow) and friends reported that he had become more impulsive and less able to control his anger after the accident.

The evidence surrounding Gage's case is limited and in recent years researchers have questioned the accuracy of some sources, but whether or not his case has been embellished or distorted, it remains the first-known reported case in which brain damage caused alterations in personality. Doctors at the time were able to hypothesize that these personality changes were a direct result of Gage's injury, meaning that this unfortunate incident pointed the way and helped us to start mapping the brain. From further case studies and by using new brain imaging techniques, we now know that the frontal lobe (which had been damaged in Gage's case) is indeed linked to controlling our impulses, which can vary from resisting the urge to devour another biscuit to the compulsive behaviours that are seen in disorders such as Obsessive Compulsive Disorder (OCD) and addiction.

The lobes of the brain

Each lobe of the brain is associated with a different function.

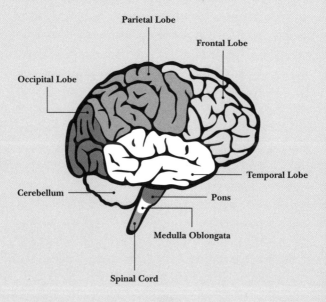

Parietal Lobe

Frontal Lobe

Occipital Lobe

Temporal Lobe

Cerebellum

Pons

Medulla Oblongata

Spinal Cord

There are four lobes that make up the human brain: the frontal, temporal, parietal and occipital lobes. Each of these lobes is associated with specific functions. The **frontal lobe** is responsible for our executive functions, the higher-level processes that allow us to make decisions, think creatively and initiate or inhibit actions. In the **temporal lobe**, memories and language are processed for understanding, while the **parietal lobe** helps us perceive, interpret and make sense of the world. Finally, the **occipital lobe** processes information from our eyes, splitting it into smaller categories such as visual tone, pattern and distance.

There is also an area of the occipital lobe dedicated to recognizing faces, which explains our talent for seeing faces in the patterns of clouds or burnt pieces of toast! Two strips along the top of the brain receive signals from specific parts of the body, processing movement and sensation. If a person suffers an injury and loses a limb, it is the corresponding parts of the motor and sensory cortex that undergo extreme remapping and, for example, can result in "phantom limb" syndrome in amputees.

Signals are transferred within and between these lobes from all over the body through neurons. Neurons are cells that are specially adapted to carry the electrical impulses that allow us to think and feel. These electrical impulses are conducted along neurons at a speed of up to 119 metres per second, passing messages from our sense organs, such as the skin, eyes and nose, to our brains, to be interpreted and acted upon. Electrical impulses pass between neurons with the help of neurotransmitters, which are chemical messengers that can travel across the synapse (the small gap) between one neuron and another. You may have heard of neurotransmitters such as serotonin or dopamine, which are associated with various cognitive functions such as happiness, memory, attention and so on.

THE STRUCTURE OF A NEURON

Impulses travel through the neuron from the dendrites to the axon terminals. The word "dendrite" comes from the Greek meaning "tree", as they are small branches projecting from a neuron that connect with the axon terminals of neighbouring neurons. Axon terminals release neurotransmitters (such as dopamine and serotonin) that carry the impulses across the synapse (the small gap between dendrites and axon terminals) and are then received by the dendrite of the next neuron, where the journey begins again.

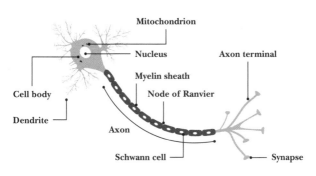

Neuromyth: "We only use 10 per cent of our brains."

FALSE!

We use all of our brains all of the time, although some areas might be working harder than others depending on the task we are doing.

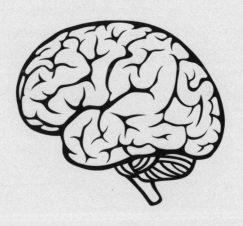

IN THE LAST ANALYSIS THE
ENTIRE FIELD OF PSYCHOLOGY
MAY REDUCE TO BIOLOGICAL
ELECTROCHEMISTRY.

SIGMUND FREUD

Wrapped across the entire surface of the brain are folds and fissures creating an immense surface area that, without a blood supply, appears grey. This is due to the huge amount of myelin sheath, a fatty wrap around these elongated neurons that helps to conduct the electrical signals travelling across your brain. As you read this, pathways of electrical signals are travelling between all of your lobes, creating memories and linking to previous processing, without you feeling like you are waiting on any kind of information retrieval. It is beautifully connected.

Our amazing and complicated brains never stop learning. The brain constantly adapts to our demanding environments, reallocating its resources depending on what we are asking it to do. For example, studies have shown that when people learn demanding tasks, such as how to juggle or play video games, the structures of their brains actually change as a result of these activities. For instance, London taxi drivers have been found to have an enlarged area of the brain known as the hippocampus. The hippocampus is associated with memory, and taxi drivers certainly need reliable memories when negotiating the winding streets of London.

AN EVOLUTIONARY PERSPECTIVE

Changes to the brain have occurred over a much longer time, too. Evolutionary psychologists would suggest that current human behaviour is a response to the pressures we were under during our early evolution, and many of our behaviours were developed through natural selection to help us survive in our environment of evolutionary adaptiveness. Humans appear to have changed very little in the last 100,000 years, so considering what might have been a behavioural advantage for our ancestors during this time could give us an insight into the original purposes of our current behaviours.

Darwin's theory of natural selection suggests that the organisms that are best suited to their environment will survive and reproduce, passing their successful traits on to their offspring. To understand the evolutionary approach in psychology, we have to be aware of what this early environment was like, and understand how it is different from the ways we live now. We have to assume that many of our current behaviours were at one point adaptive in helping us with our need to pass on our genes in this environment.

This is a concept that Richard Dawkins famously referred to as "the selfish gene". For example, it may seem obvious that for our genes to be passed on our offspring must survive, and therefore many of the maternal and paternal feelings we have towards our children are clearly an adaptive advantage. However, what might be less obvious is why we would choose to help others and behave altruistically. What possible evolutionary advantage could there be in that?

Well, it could be that cooperating with others, whether they are directly related to us or not, helps us all in the long run. We benefit from working with other members of our species to help us survive, so even behaviours that do not obviously seem to fit the pattern of "the selfish gene" may ultimately be influenced by our evolutionary past. During our early evolution we may have benefitted from dividing our food fairly, communicating goals and strategies, sharing knowledge and supporting our group. The individuals who were able to behave in such a "co-operative" way would have had an advantage over others, and therefore would have been more likely to survive, breed and pass on their seemingly altruistic genes to the next generation.

The future of this area of psychology is very exciting. More portable versions of MRI scanners are being developed, which will allow us to scan the brains of patients in battlefields or in remote hospitals in poorer countries. Researchers at the University of Nottingham are working on creating wearable brain scanning equipment that uses quantum sensors to help us detect and precisely map the tiniest changes in the electrical signals that are our thoughts. Implanted man-made diamonds may be able to bridge missing or damaged neural connections, due to the diamonds' superconducting properties, allowing the electrical nerve impulse to be carried forward where the neural pathway has been broken. This could possibly even allow us to reverse neurodegenerative disorders.

In the last few years scientists from the University of Cambridge were the first to be able to grow cerebral cortex cells (the brain's "grey matter") from a sample of skin cells. This allowed them to watch diseases such as Alzheimer's develop in real time, to develop drugs to combat these diseases and to potentially increase our understanding of how the brain recovers its ability to function after injury. Scientists at the Yale School of Medicine have also been able to use these "micro" brains to investigate how the brains of people with autism develop differently from the brains of non-autistic individuals.

Our understanding of the biology of our brain and behaviour is likely to increase hugely in the next few decades, alongside advances in other areas of biology, and what we discover is very likely to be both fascinating and awe-inspiring.

The Psychodynamic Approach

Sigmund Freud (1856–1939) is arguably the most famous psychologist of all. The image of Freud psychoanalysing a patient while they recline on a couch is synonymous with psychological therapy. He is tremendously well known outside his own field and has contributed many phrases and new word meanings to the English language, despite most of his major works being written originally in German. The concept of a "Freudian slip" is well known, and Freud is also credited with providing the first-known example of the use of the word "anxiety" to describe "a morbid state of mind", in his 1909 work on hysteria.

However, despite his major contributions to the study of the mind, many of Freud's concepts and theories have fallen out of fashion. They are accused of being male-centred, representing a Victorian-era view of sexuality, with many of his theories being untestable and therefore unfalsifiable (meaning that they cannot be scientifically proven or disproven). In this chapter, we will explore some of Freud's major theories and discuss the impact that they have had on the study of the mind.

THE MIND IS LIKE AN ICEBERG. IT FLOATS WITH ONE-SEVENTH OF ITS BULK ABOVE WATER.

SIGMUND FREUD

Sigmund Freud was born the eldest of eight children in Moravia (now the Czech Republic) on 6 May 1856 to Jewish parents. In 1860 his family moved to Vienna, where his father, a wool merchant, sought new business opportunities in order to support his young family. Freud had ambitions to become a lawyer and go into politics; however, after graduating from school he decided to turn his attention to his "urge to understand something about the mysteries of the world and maybe contribute somewhat to their understanding".

At the age of 17 he attended the University of Vienna Medical School, publishing his first paper about the sexual organs of eels in 1877 (maybe a hint about some of his future theories of the mind!). After graduating, Freud specialized in researching the brain and nervous system at the Vienna General Hospital, and later, as an intern in Paris, he went on to develop an interest in the use of hypnosis to treat hysteria and neurosis. He opened his own practice in 1886, specializing in nervous disorders; and, ten years later, in 1896, the death of his father encouraged Freud to study his own dreams, leading to the publication of his famous work *The Interpretation of Dreams* in 1900.

In 1902 Freud took a post as Professor of Neuropathology at the University of Vienna, where he met other like-minded academics. He was part of several groups that met to discuss the analysis of the mind. Each Wednesday he would invite a small group of physicians to meet in his apartment and discuss psychology and neuropathology (creatively named the Psychological Wednesday Society). This group later developed into the Vienna Psychoanalytical Society and later the International Psychoanalytic Association (IPA), which still exists today. Famous people in psychology have been president of this association at various times, including its first president, Carl Jung.

Carl Jung (1875–1961) was a Swiss psychiatrist and psychoanalyst, who was 19 years younger than Freud. The two met in 1907 after Jung sent Freud some of his work and, after a short exchange of letters, Jung travelled to Vienna. It is reported that they hit it off immediately and spent around 13 hours straight discussing psychology on their first meeting.

The two men collaborated and delivered lecture tours together, with Freud commenting that Jung was like a son he could pass the reins of psychoanalysis on to (despite the fact he already had a wife and six children). However, in 1912, on a lecture tour of America, a feud developed and broke their relationship after Jung publicly criticized Freud's theory of the Oedipus complex. In his 1914 work *The History of the Psychoanalytic Movement*, Freud delegitimized Jung's contributions. Some report that this parting was ultimately due to differences of opinion regarding the psychoanalytic approach; others claim that there were more personal reasons for the break. Regardless of the reasoning, Freud's and Jung's theories were irreversibly intertwined and have many similarities and divergences that we will discuss in this chapter.

The start of World War One halted the work of the IPA and Freud. In 1933, the Nazis began burning copies of Freud's published works and Freud fled Vienna for London, where a replica of his Vienna consulting room was set up for him to continue practising. After the war, Freud's work concentrated mostly on developing his theories and using them to analyse works of art and literature. He died in 1939, aged 83, not because of the cancer from which he was suffering, but due to receiving an overdose of morphine from his personal physician. He left a lifetime of work that had, and is still having, a significant impact on the field of psychology – and beyond.

To understand Freud's view of behaviour we need to remind ourselves of the biological approach he took to psychology. As a teenager Freud bought a first edition copy of Darwin's *On the Origin of Species*, and was fascinated by the concept of evolution by natural selection. If physical traits could be passed on to future generations, why not psychological ones? Freud believed that much of our behaviour is the result of unconscious, biological urges that are mediated by our conscious mind. This is the basis for what is known as the tripartite personality, which consists of the Id, the Superego and the Ego.

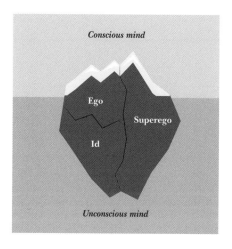

The **Id** exists in our unconscious mind and represents our instinctual, biological urges. It consists of two major parts (both named after figures in Greek mythology): Eros, the life (or sexual) instincts, and Thanatos, the death instincts. The Id encourages us to be impulsive, take what we want and do what we want. Freud believed that all children are born with a fully developed Id, and this encourages them to seek out their basic needs, such as food, in order to survive.

The **Superego** is also largely in our unconscious mind, but it can influence our conscious thought. It represents the moral principles that are learned during childhood – meaning that we are not born with a fully functioning Superego. It is developed through interaction with our family and society. The Superego is formed of two parts: the conscience and the ideal self. If we do not live up to the idealized moral principles of the Superego, we experience guilt and shame.

Finally, we have the **Ego**. The Ego represents our conscious self, and mediates impulses from the Id and moral reasoning from the Superego. The Ego is ruled by the "reality principle". This means that it tries to work out realistic ways to satisfy the Id's demands, while also being able to function in society. If we obeyed all of the demands of the Id our behaviour would be impulsive and chaotic, so the Ego ensures that this doesn't happen.

Freud believed that the Id and the Superego, existing in the unconscious mind, are in constant conflict as they try to influence the Ego, in the conscious mind. A psychologically healthy person will be able to mediate the influences of the Id and Superego. A psychologically unhealthy person may have an Id or Superego that is overactive, that they cannot satisfy, which can result in anxiety and other mental health issues. It is easy to consider the Id and Superego as the little devil and angel often shown on the shoulders of cartoon protagonists, willing them to be naughty or nice. If one has more power than the other, the Ego is left confused and defenceless.

The Ego needs to protect itself from the sometimes unreasonable demands from the Id and Superego, and it does so by using defence mechanisms. Freud believed that we are unaware that these mechanisms are taking effect, but their influence can be uncovered using therapies such as the analysis of dreams. If you have ever been told that you are in denial, or that you are repressing an emotion, then you have certainly heard of some of these mechanisms before. The following table lists four of the more common examples of defence mechanisms; however they are not limited to just these four.

DEFENCE MECHANISM	DESCRIPTION	EXAMPLE
Repression	When traumatic or disturbing thoughts are blocked from consciousness.	Not being able to remember childhood abuse or bullying.
Denial	When the mind refuses to accept a reality or fact, and an individual continues as if that reality or fact does not exist.	Refusing to accept that you are suffering from a terminal illness.
Projection	When an individual's own unacceptable thoughts are attributed to another person.	Imagining that you do not get on with someone because they hate you, when in fact it is you who dislikes them.
Displacement	When unacceptable thoughts or impulses are directed onto another, less threatening, person or object.	Smashing a cup instead of hitting a person you are arguing with.

Although we are born with a fully formed Id, our Ego and Superego develop as we grow. Freud believed that they develop as we pass through what he called "psychosexual stages" and that we are supported through these stages by our parents. They are called psychosexual stages as they are thought to be linked to the development of our sexual drive, or "libido". If we become fixated, or stuck, at a stage it can influence our adult behaviour. For example, if a person becomes fixated at the oral stage, they may bite their nails as an adult. Of course we are not aware of experiencing these stages, as Freud believed that these mechanisms existed in the unconscious mind.

STAGE	EROGENOUS ZONE	KEY EVENTS	PROBLEMS FROM FIXATION
Oral 0–1 year old	Mouth	Sucking, chewing and biting, and experiencing breastfeeding and weaning	Smoking, nail-biting and gluttony
Anal 1–3 years old	Anus	Urination and defecation, and experiencing potty training	Overly messy or overly controlling
Phallic 3–6 years old	Genitals	Genital stimulation and experiencing the Oedipus and Electra (see page 37) complexes	Jealousy, vanity and unhealthy sexual desires
Latent 6–12 years old	None	Acquiring an understanding of the world	No fixations at this stage
Genital 12 years old onwards	Genitals		No fixations at this stage

Freud's theories regarding the phallic stage of psychosexual development are particularly interesting. During this stage children begin to notice physical differences between the sexes, and our parents are also thought to help us come to terms with one of two rather controversial complexes: the Oedipus complex in boys and the Electra complex in girls.

When experiencing the Oedipus complex, boys wish to possess their mothers and replace their fathers. They feel as though their father is a rival, but they also fear that they will be punished by their fathers for these feelings, which is known as castration anxiety.

During the Electra complex (a concept first introduced by Freud's contemporary, Carl Jung, and disputed by Freud), a girl is thought to have "penis envy". She notices that she does not have a penis, while the male members of her family do, and she wishes that she too had one. Freud thought that the girl's logical reasoning would be to believe that her mother had cut off her, the girl's, penis. Once the girl realizes it isn't possible for her to have a penis, she represses her rage against the mother and replaces her desire for a penis with a desire to have a baby.

If a boy successfully passes through the phallic stage and resolves his Oedipus complex, he will begin to imitate his father by displaying typically masculine behaviours. Girls, however, according to Freud, never fully resolve their penis envy. This point was scathingly criticized by German psychoanalyst **Karen Horney** (1885-1952), who found the concept that women were defined by their jealousy of male genitals offensive. She dismissed Freud's concept of penis envy and stated that it was developed due to misplaced "masculine narcissism".

Jung also disagreed with Freud's theory of the Oedipus complex. He felt that it was "unnecessarily negative" and incomplete. While Freud and Jung agreed that the unconscious mind influences our behaviour, and that past experiences may be repressed, Jung noted that future aspirations also influence behaviour, and that the libido was not just specific to sexual gratification but motivated by a range of behaviours.

While Jung agreed that the human psyche was composed of the Id and the unconscious, he believed that there was more to our unconscious than Freud had described. Jung thought that, alongside our personal unconscious (the temporarily forgotten information and repressed memories of our own past), there was also a level of collective unconscious that is shared between all humans. According to Jung, this collective unconscious includes innate memories from our ancestral past, images and thoughts that form a human psyche based on our evolutionary origins. Jung named these "archetypes".

Jung used the concept of innate, universal and hereditary archetypes to explain common human concepts that span different cultures, such as religion and morality. Some examples might also include common phobias, such as a fear of spiders. Jung believed that a limitless number of archetypes may exist, but argued that there are four major examples, which are summarized below.

The Persona

Derived from the Latin word for "mask", this archetype represents the different metaphorical social masks we wear in different situations. Children learn that they are expected to behave differently in different social situations, so this archetype allows people to adapt to the world around them.

The Shadow

Similar to the Id in many ways, the shadow includes the primal sex and life instincts. It contains all of the desires that are unacceptable in society and to a person's own morality. Jung thought that this archetype existed in the unconscious but may manifest in dreams, represented by a monster or demon.

The Anima/Animus

This archetype is related to our biological gender, with the anima representing feminine aspects of the male psyche, and the animus representing male aspects of the female psyche. This archetype is influenced by the collective unconscious, but also by gender socialization as a child grows. Jung argued that if people were forced to conform to strict gender roles and were not allowed to explore the opposite-sex aspects of the psyche it would negatively affect their psychological development.

The Self
This archetype represents a person's unified psyche, including both the conscious and the unconscious mind. The self is the centre of a person's *personality* whereas Jung considered the Ego as the centre of the conscious mind.

There are other areas where Freud and Jung's approaches differ. For example, Jung placed an emphasis on "parapsychology" and "psychic phenomena", whereas Freud felt that trying to explain such experiences cast psychoanalysis in a negative light, deviating from the scientific community. Despite their eventual differences, Freud and Jung have each had an immeasurable impact on our understanding of psychology and the development of future theories.

It is important to mention here that these theories were developed during the Victorian era, where the stereotypes of the mother as caregiver and the father as breadwinner were the norm. There was an assumption that heterosexual relationships were "normal" and functional, and that this was what males and females should be striving to achieve. It is also important to note that Freud's theories represent a male perspective of both male and female psychology, and many of his theories are unfalsifiable. However, despite these shortcomings, the impact of Freud and Jung's theories on the study of psychology is undeniable. Freud was one of the first to highlight the relationship between childhood experiences and adult behaviour, and one of the first to connect our behaviour with innate, biological drives. Overall, Freud presented a sometimes fantastical, but ultimately groundbreaking analysis of the human mind.

The Behaviourist Approach

Whatever your memories, the behaviourist approach would suggest that the lessons you had in school were not where you did most of your learning. A behavioural psychologist would suggest that your current behaviours are the result of all of your previous experiences. These experiences will have taught you what to do (or feel), based on observation, imitation, and possibly reinforcement or punishment. This approach to the study of behaviour has taught us a lot about how humans and animals learn. It has contributed to the development of some highly effective treatments for phobias and has been used in a wide range of fields, including the training of animals, behaviour management in education and sports psychology. This chapter will look at theories behind how we learn from experience.

**EDUCATION SURVIVES WHEN
WHAT HAS BEEN LEARNT
HAS BEEN FORGOTTEN.**

B. F. SKINNER

In the 1890s, **Ivan Pavlov** (1849-1936) accidentally stumbled upon a vital learning theory, in what would go on to be perhaps one of the most well-known psychological experiments of all time. He was conducting a set of ethically dubious physiological experiments to investigate digestive function in dogs (for which he won a Nobel Prize in 1904), and in one experiment was measuring the amount of saliva a dog produces when it is presented with food. He measured this very precisely, by drilling into the dogs' salivary glands and implanting a cannula with a vial attached, which would catch any saliva produced by the dogs. Salivation is an example of a reflex action, a response that the dogs did not learn or control – it just happened whenever they saw the tasty meat powder that their handlers brought them. However, it seemed that the dogs also drooled at all the cues that led up to their dinner too, for example, the sound of their handler's footsteps or a glimpse of a white lab coat. While any pet owner will confirm that even the slight tinkling of a biscuit tin will elicit an enthusiastic response from a previously asleep and un-drooling Labrador, it was Pavlov who applied the scientific method to observe cause and effect to explain this behaviour. He took this opportunity to research how we can learn to associate one thing with another, often without realizing. This is known as "classical conditioning".

Classical conditioning is essentially learning through association. During classical conditioning, two stimuli are repeatedly paired with each other until they become associated with one another. Eventually, a response that was previously only associated with one stimulus is now associated with both.

For example, in Pavlov's case he had two stimuli. One was the unconditioned stimulus, the food. He called it "unconditioned" because the dogs responded to this stimulus without being taught (or "conditioned") to. This unconditioned stimulus created an unconditioned response: salivating. The second stimulus was a buzzer, known as the "neutral" stimulus. He called this neutral because it was not previously associated with the other stimulus. What Pavlov then did was to repeatedly pair these two stimuli, food and buzzer, until the dogs began to realize that the sound of a buzzer meant that food was coming. Once this association had been made, the dogs would salivate at the sound of the buzzer without any food present at all. The salivation response was what he now called the "conditioned response", as the dogs had been conditioned to associate the buzzer with food, and therefore to respond by salivating.

Classical conditioning happens to both humans and animals regularly without us realizing it. It is because of this learned association that people often feel hungry when watching television, or why the Labrador in our example above has learned to associate the sound of their biscuit tin (or your biscuit tin!) with a delicious treat. It can be used to our advantage when training animals, but can also be to our disadvantage when trying to kick bad habits.

In the diagram below you will see that we have included a bell as the neutral stimulus, as is common in diagrams of Pavlov's experiment, but Pavlov actually used a buzzer or a metronome. A mistranslation of the original Russian at some point in history means that most people incorrectly learn that this study took place using a bell.

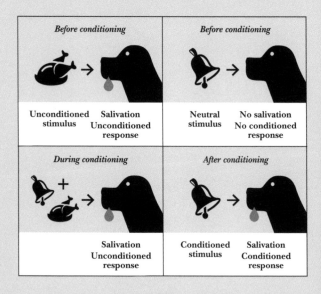

Before conditioning	*Before conditioning*
Unconditioned stimulus — Salivation Unconditioned response	Neutral stimulus — No salivation No conditioned response
During conditioning	*After conditioning*
Salivation Unconditioned response	Conditioned stimulus — Salivation Conditioned response

CONDITIONING HUMANS

In 1920, **John B. Watson** (1878–1958) built on Pavlov's work by investigating if these principles would apply to humans. In a controversial study conducted with his colleague Rosalie Rayner (whom he later married), an infant known in the study as Albert B. was intentionally conditioned to be fearful of small animals.

Albert B. (now thought to have actually been called Douglas Merritte) was the nine-month-old child of a wet nurse who worked at the same hospital as Watson and Rayner. Reports differ, with some suggestion that Albert's mother was unaware of the exact procedures that her child was experiencing, but most recent evidence suggests that she willingly allowed her child's participation in the investigation due to the fact that Watson and Rayner claimed to have measures in place to reverse the conditioning that occurred.

Albert was subjected to a series of different conditions, beginning with being exposed to an array of objects in order to gauge his emotional reaction and ensure that he was emotionally stable. These included various animals (a white rat, a rabbit, a dog, a monkey), masks with and without hair, wool, burning newspapers and other objects. Albert had normal emotional reactions to these objects and did not display obvious signs of fear, confirming that any fear he had of the objects in later weeks must have been due to the scary procedures he was about to experience. In fact, Watson and Rayner specifically chose Albert on account of his "stolid and unemotional" nature.

When he was 11 months old, Albert was brought back to the hospital. This time, when Albert was presented with the white rat and reached out to play with it, Watson and Rayner struck a steel bar with a hammer to make a loud noise right behind him. The noise frightened Albert, causing him to cry and try to move away. This procedure was repeated over the next few weeks, pairing the loud noise with the white rat until Albert made an association between the two. Eventually Albert learned to associate the white rat with the unpleasant noise and would recoil, turn away and cry when the rat was shown to him. Over the coming weeks Watson and Rayner continued to study Albert, and found that he had also become fearful of objects that were similar to the white rat, such as a fur coat or a white beard. They conducted most of their procedures in a well-lit darkroom (a darkroom used to develop photographs or X-rays, not a room that could somehow be simultaneously dark and well-lit at the same time!), but found that he would still be fearful of these objects when he was taken to a different room (a large, bright lecture room), showing that Albert could generalize his fear to different situations. They also found that he showed fear after he had not seen the objects for about a month, although in both of these conditions he was less fearful than he had been before.

Unfortunately both Albert and his mother moved away before the investigation could be completed and Watson and Rayner did not get the opportunity to fulfil their promise of reversing the conditioning that Albert had experienced. It is now thought that Albert sadly died of encephalitis at a young age, so we do not know how long the fear conditioning lasted or whether it could have developed into a lifelong phobia. But we do know from countless other studies that a learned response can be generalized to other situations and objects (for example, if you are scared of the movement of a spider, you may be scared by the movement of a crab), and the fear can also become naturally extinct (forgotten) over time.

It is believed that a learned response such as this can develop into a phobia – a persistent and irrational fear that interferes with everyday life. Psychologists can use a treatment called systematic desensitization to help a patient to relearn their responses to stimuli, essentially by replacing one conditioned response (for example, fear) with a new, less stressful, conditioned response (relaxation).

SYSTEMATIC DESENSITIZATION

During systematic desensitization, the phobia in question is broken down into different levels or steps that become increasingly scary for the patient (a desensitization hierarchy), and each level is paired with a relaxation technique such as controlled breathing. If we take the example of a phobia of spiders, the steps might be:

1. Touch a picture of a spider while practising a relaxation technique.
2. Be in the same room as a spider while practising a relaxation technique.
3. Touch a dead spider while practising a relaxation technique.
4. Stand next to a live spider while practising a relaxation technique.
5. Touch a live spider while practising a relaxation technique.
6. Hold a live spider while practising a relaxation technique.

Eventually the patient learns to associate the fearful stimulus (in this example, a spider) with a new response: that of feeling relaxed. Because of a concept known as reciprocal inhibition (the inability to feel two opposing emotions, such as fear and relaxation, at the same time), the patient will no longer feel fearful in the presence of their phobic stimulus.

The benefit of this treatment is that each stage is decided with the patient; they can set their own limits and return to earlier stages if needed. Relearning a response to a stimulus has a higher success rate than other treatments such as flooding (immersing someone in their fearful situation), but it does not work for everyone, and isn't appropriate for all types of phobia.

In 1938, American psychologist (and later Harvard professor) **B. F. Skinner** (1904–1990) proposed a new theory of learning known as "operant conditioning". He theorized that we learn new behaviours based on whether our actions are punished or rewarded. Behaviour that is immediately followed by a positive consequence is likely to be repeated, but if it is followed by a negative consequence, it is likely to be extinguished (or weakened).

For example, when you were at school, perhaps you spent some time drawing a particularly nice graph and your teacher rewarded your efforts with credits, a sticker, or even simple verbal praise, thus causing you to repeat this behaviour and starting your enthusiastic graph-drawing career. On the other hand, maybe there was a time when you didn't hand in your homework on time (maybe one of Pavlov's dogs ate it?) and you were given a detention. As a result of this you have diligently met every single deadline you have ever come across since. Perhaps you are not overly attached to the 100-credit certificate you were once awarded in assembly, but perhaps you are excited at the prospect of a promotion or bonus at work. Same system, different age groups (although if our bosses gave out stickers too, we would probably spend a little less time at work making coffee!).

Skinner actually had little interest in becoming a psychologist until he was in his early twenties and happened to read an essay written by H. G. Wells, which appeared in *Time* magazine. It was about Ivan Pavlov and his experiments with classical conditioning, applauding his systematic study of human reflexes. Skinner went on to idolize Pavlov. In August 1929, at the age of 25, he was lucky enough to attend a talk given by Pavlov at the Harvard Medical School, where he bought a signed photograph of his idol. He carried this photograph with him throughout his life, hanging it in his various offices until it finally found its way to his home in Cambridge. When writing, in 1979, about his time as a student, Skinner said "I began to build a library, starting with Bertrand Russell's *Philosophy*, John B. Watson's *Behaviorism*, and I. P. Pavlov's *Conditioned Reflexes* – the books which had, I thought, prepared me for a career in psychology."

Skinner is best known for developing this theory through his laboratory work with rats, rewarding them with treats when they pressed a lever. However, during World War Two, he worked on Project Orcon. This ambitious project planned to use his theory of operant conditioning to develop a missile piloted by the learned behaviour of a pigeon. Using reward-based operant conditioning, the pigeons were trained to peck at specific shapes on a screen, the intention being that they could be placed in a compartment in the nose cone of a missile and, using sensors, guide the missile towards a target. Sadly for Skinner, but luckily for the pigeons, this project was abandoned after electronic guidance systems were improved and were shown to work reliably.

Pavlov and Skinner were on to something, but they had not considered how we can also learn things just by observing other people. Nor did they focus their attention on the processes that could be taking place between stimulus and response. Enter **Albert Bandura** (1925-) in 1977, who identified that we are constantly observing the behaviours of others. Those who we particularly identify with are called "models" – not the ridiculously good-looking kind, although this theory can be applied in arguments for realistic representation in advertising, particularly when we want to develop things like positive body image for teenagers.

Bandura conducted a series of experiments showing that children who watched an adult "model" hit a Bobo doll (an inflatable clown that rocks backwards and forwards when it is struck) were likely to repeat the aggressive behaviour. However, if they observed the model treating the doll nicely, then they would do the same. What was particularly interesting was that this imitation was more common if the model was the same gender as the child observer. Furthermore, when the children observed a model being rewarded for a behaviour, they were even more likely to imitate the behaviour themselves.

For example, perhaps you witnessed your parents praising your brother or sister for playing nicely, and copied the behaviour yourself. Prior to Bandura's research, it was believed that watching aggressive behaviour on television or in sports was cathartic and cleansed us of our own aggressive urges. Now new concerns were raised over the role television may have been playing in the development of young minds.

If you reconsider these theories of learning you can probably identify a behaviour of your own that is paired with a neutral stimulus or has been reinforced with a reward, or a behaviour you have avoided for which you can recall seeing someone else get punished. Maybe you can't remember the exact circumstances that led to you avoiding stepping on cracks in the pavement, or purposely wearing your lucky pair of pants on your driving test, but the fact that this behaviour removes some of the unpleasant feeling of worry might be the reinforcing factor that causes you to keep doing it.

Some psychologists suggest that we can use behavioural theory to explain why we like some foods and not others: for example, that time the risk of eating out-of-date prawns didn't pay off, and now your brain has linked the feelings of sickness with your former favourite food. Some learned behaviours are less obvious and can be used to manipulate us. Time spent posting on social media can be associated with the positive consequences of approval and attention, encouraging the behaviour to be repeated, perhaps to the detriment of other things. This example has similarities with those from addiction psychology, and also the study and treatment of phobias. What makes one reward better than another? What causes a well-learned behaviour to become extinct? Behaviour is complex – is it too reductionist to say that we have simply learned it?

Because behavioural psychologists are interested in observing cause and effect it is considered to be one of the more traditionally scientific areas of psychology, where clear variables can be established and then responses easily measured. They investigate how a stimulus from the environment can create a behavioural response. But what they do not consider is what happens in between the two – the thought processes that mediate these behaviours. Which brings us to our next chapter...

The Cognitive Approach

Behavioural psychologists reacted to the subjective conclusions of the psychodynamic approach by studying behaviour in a very objective, scientific way. They focused on manipulating a stimulus and observing a response, measuring cause and effect with straightforward observations. But their methods do not allow us to inspect the *thought processes* behind our actions. The reaction to this was the cognitive approach. Cognitive psychologists wanted to go beyond simply trying to observe stimulus and response; they were looking to explain what happens in between. In this chapter we will look at how this branch of psychology has used scientific methods to make sense of what goes on inside our heads between the observable cause and effect.

Research in the field of cognitive psychology looks at a very wide range of processes that you probably don't pay much attention to as you go about your day-to-day life, but you would most definitely notice if they stopped running properly. This field of psychology aims to understand those higher-level procedures that make us who we are. For example, how we use language, how we solve problems or how we create memories.

There is no shortage of information coming into our brains from the outside world (referred to as "external stimuli"), and some cognitive psychologists would argue that the brain deals with this information like a computer, receiving input (external stimuli), processing it (cognition) and then producing output (behaviour or emotions). The brain efficiently encodes information, retrieving files and storing new ones, while prioritizing which functions to work on immediately and which can be ignored or just run in the background. The cognitive approach looks at how these systems run, and what happens when they don't.

Explaining how these cognitive processes develop was the life's work of psychologist **Jean Piaget** (1896–1980). Born in Switzerland, Piaget was fascinated by biology and nature as a child. When he was only ten years old his first article was published, a description of an albino sparrow. Before he was 18 years old, several of his papers about molluscs had been published by scientific journals. He went on to study zoology at the University of Neuchâtel, before working at the University of Zurich in Bleuler's Psychiatric Clinic, where he developed an interest in psychology. This led him to study clinical psychology at the Sorbonne in Paris in 1919. Piaget was also very interested in a branch of philosophy known as epistemology (the study of knowledge and rational beliefs), and this combination of interests and experiences led him to develop theories of learning (which combine biology and psychology, and focus on how we acquire knowledge) that are still influential today.

In 1920 Piaget was working in the laboratories of the famous psychologists Alfred Binet and Theodore Simon in Paris. Binet and Simon were funded by the French government to seek ways to help children who were struggling in education, and they are credited with inventing standardized IQ testing with their first intelligence test (the "Binet–Simon" test) being published in 1905. During Piaget's time in Paris, Theodore Simon was using intelligence tests to see if children of similar ages made similar errors in their reasoning. Piaget however was more interested in *why* the children gave incorrect answers, and asked them to explain their reasoning after they had completed the tests. He found that the children had used logical reasoning to come to their conclusions, but did not have enough life experience to know all of the correct answers, so would fill in the gaps using their imagination. As well as being a key indication that intelligence and knowledge are not the same thing, this also gave Piaget clues about how our logical reasoning develops.

In the coming years Piaget continued to observe children and investigate how they make judgements and how they explain them, eventually writing more than 50 books and publishing hundreds of articles. Although Piaget aimed to develop a scientific approach to understanding the development of knowledge, and approved of Binet and Simon's methods, his methods of observation were more complex and his researchers had to be trained for an entire year before they were ready to collect any data. He went on to develop several theories explaining how children develop, which he called "genetic epistemology", or "a developmental theory of knowledge". Essentially, Piaget believed that children develop knowledge through interaction with their surroundings, and that this knowledge is constantly being added to and adjusted. He thought that there were three main areas of knowledge acquisition:

1. Physical knowledge (knowledge about physical objects)
2. Logical-mathematical knowledge (knowledge about abstract concepts)
3. Social-arbitrary knowledge (knowledge about culturally specific concepts)

Piaget also believed that children go through four stages of development in order to acquire knowledge about the world: the sensorimotor, pre-operational, concrete operational and formal operational stages. All children pass through these stages in the same order, but not necessarily at the same ages, and this progression can be influenced by many factors, such as culture, biological development and so on. Each stage is outlined in more detail in the table below.

STAGE	AGE RANGE	DESCRIPTION
Sensorimotor	Birth–2 years	Children begin to explore the world using their senses, such as touch. They begin to develop object permanence (realizing that objects do not disappear when they cannot see them).
Pre-operational	2–7 years	Children learn to represent the world using words and images. Their language abilities develop and they begin to use imaginary and pretend play. They are egocentric and see the world predominantly from their own point of view.
Concrete operational	7–11 years	Children begin to think logically. They understand that objects can change in shape but still have the same volume (conservation), and can start to use mathematical concepts. They understand the concept of cause and effect.

Formal operational	11 years +	Children can now use abstract thinking strategies and consider hypothetical scenarios. They can start to reason using concepts such as morality, and can use deductive reasoning.

Piaget thought that we progress through these stages as we mature biologically and build up knowledge from our environment. At each stage we create little packets of information that tell us how the world works, known as schemas, and we constantly adapt these schemas as we go through new experiences, using processes known as *organization, adaptation, assimilation* and *accommodation*. Organization is our ability to coordinate existing schemas and combine them into more complex behaviours. For example, a baby may combine the schemas for looking, reaching, grasping and sucking in order to feed itself. When we experience something new, we *assimilate* this new information into our schemas. If we then have a new experience and find that our current schemas don't quite work, we experience *disequilibrium* and need to *accommodate* this new information into our current schemas. Then, we experience *equilibrium* when our schemas can handle the new information.

Many people may recognize this process happening when children learn the names of different species of animals. For example, you may have seen a scenario like this when talking to a child:

Assimilation: A child experiences seeing a duck, and their parent says, "Look! A duck." The child has now built a schema for a duck, which may include the facts that a duck has feathers, wings and a beak.

Disequilibrium: A child sees another animal with wings, feathers and a beak. It's a pigeon. They say to their parent, "Look! A duck." Their parent tells them no, that is a different type of bird called a pigeon. The child is experiencing disequilibrium - their schema for a duck didn't work this time.

Accommodation: The child accommodates this new information into their schema. Birds all have wings, feathers and beaks, but the grey birds are pigeons and not ducks. Ducks are the ones on the water who make the "quacking" noises.

Equilibrium: The child now has a more accurate schema for a duck as well as one for birds.

Piaget's theories of development generally see the child as a scientist who experiments with and explores the world largely independently. This contrasts with the theories of Russian psychologist **Lev Vygotsky** (1896–1934), who thought that children develop through interaction with others. Vygotsky studied law, literature and culture at the University of Moscow, moving to the Shaniavskii People's University, also in Moscow, when staff and students were expelled from the University of Moscow on suspicion of anti-tsarist activities. Vygotsky was working during a time when social scientists were under a great deal of scrutiny. They were under pressure to suppress any views that did not match the party doctrines, with Vygotsky under particular pressure after having visited several European countries during the 1920s. His best-known work, *Thought and Language*, was published in 1934 but suppressed by the Stalinist government. As a result, Vygotsky's work was largely unknown in the West until it was translated into English in the 1960s and 1970s. Unfortunately, he died of tuberculosis when he was 38 years old, so much of his work has remained unfinished.

Vygotsky differed from Piaget in that he emphasized the role of social interaction in a child's development. He believed that learning takes place when a child is supported through their zone of proximal development (ZPD) by a more knowledgeable "other", such as a parent, teacher or peer. The ZPD lies between a child's current abilities and their potential abilities. A more knowledgeable other supports the child in moving through their ZPD by deliberately challenging their abilities and understanding, but not so much as to cause the child to experience frustration or failure. The child has to have the necessary skills to meet and understand the challenge, while also being supported in order to make progress. These theories have clear implications for education and are still compulsory learning for trainee teachers in the UK.

Learner cannot do

zone of proximal development

Learner can
do unaided

learner can do with guidance

Optical illusions

What do you see below? A vase or two faces? Optical illusions such as this are the result of your brain trying to process two different pieces of information that are visually very similar.

INTERNAL MENTAL PROCESSES

We began by explaining that cognitive psychologists are interested in finding out what happens in between the stimulus and response, the processes that form our thinking. We will now look in more detail at one of the processes that we are all familiar with: memory. Your brain can probably instantly locate and retrieve your most treasured or vivid memories that are linked to strong emotions or meaningful events. But what if you were asked to list the name of every person who was in your year group at school? Or to remember exactly what you were doing at 10.50 a.m. last Tuesday? Why is it that we can remember some things so easily and not others? How do our brains prioritize some of the constant external stimuli entering our senses each day? Is it possible to remember everything, and would we even want to?

We tend to believe that we can trust our memory of events. We hold our memories in such high regard that eyewitness testimony can make or break a court case. However, evidence has shown that our memories are not reliable. We overexaggerate our own contribution to events and we will fill in gaps in our knowledge with likely, but not always correct, information. Our memories can be altered by suggestion and, as was shown in one famous study by American psychologists **Elizabeth Loftus** (1944–) and **John Palmer** (date of birth unknown), a single word can dramatically alter our recall of even a very memorable event.

In 1974 Loftus and Palmer aimed to investigate the effect of language on eyewitness testimony. They were interested in how leading questions – questions that may "lead" a witness towards a given answer, whether due to purposeful manipulation or accidental influence – could alter an eyewitness's memory of an event. They had participants watch a video recording of a car crash, and then they asked them to estimate the speed at which the cars were travelling when the accident happened. However, when they asked their question they altered the verb used to describe the accident for different participants to see if it would alter the participants' memories of the event. They were interested in the impact of five verbs in particular – smashed, collided, bumped, hit and contacted.

They found that when they asked participants "About how fast were the cars going when they *contacted* each other?" the average speed given by the participants was much lower than those who had been asked how fast the cars were going when they "*smashed into*" each other, showing that changing just one critical verb in a sentence can have a significant effect on an eyewitness's memory.

Response to the question "About how fast were the cars going when they [verb] into each other?"	
VERB USED IN CRITICAL QUESTION	AVERAGE SPEED ESTIMATE (MPH)
Smashed	40.8
Collided	39.3
Bumped	38.1
Hit	34.0
Contacted	31.8

In a second experiment, Loftus and Palmer showed a new set of participants a similar recording of a car accident and asked them at what speed the cars "smashed into" or "hit"

each other. This time they included a control group who were not asked about the speed (see table below).

A week later they questioned the same participants about whether or not they had seen any broken glass in the video, and found again that the verb that had been used a week previously had a significant effect on participants' memories.

RESPONSE	VERB CONDITION		
	SMASHED	HIT	CONTROL
Yes	16	7	6
No	34	43	44

Response to the question "Did you see any broken glass?"

Interestingly, despite there being no broken glass shown in the video at all, even some members of the control group recalled the incident incorrectly.

These experiments showed that it is not only the information gained during an experience that is important for memory, but also the information gained afterwards.

Information gained after an event can not only distort memories, but can also create new ones – in this case, participants remembering that they had seen glass when they had not. This highlights not only the danger in relying on eyewitness testimony as evidence, but also the need for very careful questioning of witnesses soon after an event to ensure that their memories are not contaminated or distorted any more than is already caused by our own minds.

MEMORY, LIKE LIBERTY, IS A FRAGILE THING.

ELIZABETH LOFTUS

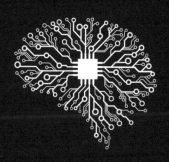

Did you know? Taking a nap could improve your memory.

In a 2008 study by Lahl *et al.* at the University of Düsseldorf, one hour after learning a list of 30 words, participants were asked to recall them. During the one-hour break they were asked to either take a nap or play a simple computer game. Recall was significantly better in the group who had taken a nap. What a great excuse next time you're caught catching some shut-eye!

Psychologists such as Loftus and Palmer found a way to study internal mental processes and how they may be influenced, but what they had not investigated was how and why these processes develop in the first place.

Cognitive psychology is concerned with how these processes (and many, many others!) develop, but to study that, researchers must try to work out when they first start to develop. You may not remember the first time you sat down to learn to read, or how you began to learn to make word sounds as an infant, but cognitive psychology seeks these answers. To do this, we must study people as they develop, beginning with very young children. However, infants are often too young to answer our questions with anything other than adorable baby sounds, so we have had to devise methods that don't rely on the very skills that we are trying to observe improving. These can involve technology such as eye trackers, or electrodes placed on the skin to record the electrical activity of the nervous system (these are known as electroencephalograms, or EEGs), or just a very well-thought-through research design. This work led to the emergence of cognitive neuroscience, where we try to match the electrical activity we are recording to behaviour. Closely tied with the biological approach, it gives us another way to study internal processes.

The work of cognitive psychologists has inspired many successful therapies, such as cognitive behavioural therapy (CBT), a therapy with a high success rate, which teaches a person how to recognize and dispute their own negative thoughts. For example, let's say that you accidentally leave your phone at home for the day. When you get home to look at it you discover that there are no messages. Not a single one. You feel upset, unpopular, alone and rejected. Why have your friends not called you? Why isn't there a message from anyone? Perhaps you don't have any friends at all and nobody likes you. This is obviously an unhealthy negative response. CBT would guide you to recognize an alternative healthy one, by examining if there is actually any evidence for your thoughts (you haven't fallen out with any of your friends, and the number of messages you receive is not a measure of how good a person you are anyway) and by suggesting other ways of thinking (perhaps your friends were just busy that day).

Techniques to dispute negative thoughts

Consider:

1. Is there any evidence for your negative belief?
2. Is your belief logical?
3. Have you had a similar belief before about a different situation?
4. Suggest three different reasonable alternatives to your negative belief.

With a growing focus on mental health in schools, the workplace and in the media, we should all be aware that having an understanding of our own thought processes can help us to live better, healthier lives. Other approaches in psychology have also developed highly effective treatments, but the cognitive approach allows us to look at the processes that lead us to certain behaviours and thoughts. The new emerging field of cognitive neuroscience is also allowing psychologists to use fMRI scanners to look at the brain while it is performing a task. We can watch maps of brain activity while someone solves a problem, focuses on a piece of music being played or experiences different emotions. fMRI stands for "functional magnetic resonance imaging", which uses a strong electromagnet to scan the brain, like an MRI, but which can also detect changes in blood flow in the brain (by calculating the amount of oxygen), so we can see which parts are working harder at any given time. As always, psychology continues to evolve and new theories are constantly being tested that will have, as yet unknown, benefits to us all.

Social Psychology

Humans are a social species. We have evolved to live in groups, and this system of living has huge benefits for us. We can support and learn from one another, forming societies and cultures that work together to share information and improve our well-being. However, living in a society also brings with it a pressure to conform. We unconsciously feel a need to be accepted by those we identify as our community, and distance ourselves from those who do not share our social norms, morals and values. This need to form social groups, which serves us well in so many ways, can therefore lead to seemingly irrational behaviour. We may outwardly conform when we inwardly feel we should not, or we may obey an authority figure even when they ask us to do something that we feel is wrong. In this chapter we will look at how psychologists have attempted to explain the principles that underlie our social behaviours, and what this can tell us about our ability to think and behave independently.

THE DISAPPEARANCE OF A SENSE OF RESPONSIBILITY IS THE MOST FAR-REACHING CONSEQUENCE OF SUBMISSION TO AUTHORITY.

STANLEY MILGRAM

Have you ever found yourself agreeing with a group of friends despite inwardly believing that they might be wrong? If so, you're not alone. In the 1950s, a Polish psychologist working in the United States, **Solomon Asch** (1907-1996), conducted a classic piece of research to investigate this behaviour, known as "conformity".

Asch wanted to investigate the human tendency to conform to the behaviour of a majority. He did this using a little deception and some rigorous standardized procedures that could leave little ambiguity regarding whether or not his participants had been influenced by their ingrained need to conform.

During the experiment, his participants (who were all white, male college students) were told that they were taking part in a study on visual perception. In groups of eight, they were asked to complete a simple task: identify which one of three lines matched a target line in length. Sounds simple? What participants did not know was that seven of the eight people in their group were actually "confederates" – actors who were in on the experiment. These confederates would give the correct answer a few times, but then begin to give incorrect answers unanimously to the simple visual task. Asch wanted to see if this clear majority of seven people could influence the answer given by the unsuspecting participant.

Asch conducted 18 trials with his participants, 12 of which were known as "critical" trials, where confederates gave the clearly incorrect answer. To check that his task wasn't too ambiguous, he also conducted several control trials where lone participants were asked the same questions, but this time without the pressure to conform to a majority as there were no confederates present. This enabled him to check that the answers really were as obvious as he thought they were.

Which line is the same size as X?

Asch found that, in the critical trials, an average of 32 per cent of the participants conformed with the clearly incorrect majority. Around 75 per cent of the participants conformed at least once during the 12 critical trials, and 25 per cent of the participants never conformed at all. In the control group, less than 1 per cent of the participants gave the wrong answer, showing that conformity in the critical trials must have been due to the majority pressure and not because the task was ambiguous.

After talking to his participants and coming clean about what they had experienced (known as "debriefing"), Asch concluded that people conform for two main reasons, "normative social influence" and "informational social influence". Some participants claimed that they wanted to fit in with the group and not be seen as unusual, a phenomenon known as normative social influence. Others doubted their own senses and claimed to really believe the group was correct. This is known as informational social influence.

While Asch's experiment does not necessarily explain why we might conform in more serious situations where moral and ethical consequences are at stake (does it really matter how long a line is?), it does give us a fascinating insight into our group dynamics. Asch followed up his original experiment with several variations, changing the order at which confederates and participants gave their answers, changing how large the majority was, and even including an ally for the participants who gave the correct answer. Through these variations Asch found that the optimum majority size is three, and adding more confederates had little additional effect. People are less likely to conform if they have an ally, and are more likely to conform if the task is more difficult.

The reasons for conforming to a group in this kind of situation might seem straightforward. Why stand out and cause disruption when so little is at stake? Even in more critical situations we can probably understand a person's reasons for conforming to a group, maybe for their own survival or safety. What is less clear is why a group of people might obey an order given by a single person, someone who is seen as an authority figure. There are many instances in human history where irrational or horrendous acts have been committed by groups of people at the request of one or a few leaders. One of the most famous attempts to explain this phenomenon is what we will look at next.

The experiment on obedience that **Stanley Milgram** (1933-1984) carried out during the 1960s is one of the most controversial studies in this area of psychology. Milgram wanted to investigate why ordinary people may do extraordinarily terrible things when under the influence of an authority figure. He had a particular interest in confessions made following World War Two, where Nazi soldiers would claim that they only committed horrendous acts against their captives because they were "following orders" from their superiors.

Milgram investigated this phenomenon by asking volunteer participants to take part in what they were told was an experiment on learning. The participants were to act as teachers, and were told to subject "learners" to increasingly powerful electric shocks every time they answered a question incorrectly. To encourage participants to do this Milgram simply had to have an "authority figure"

present in the room. This person would be wearing a white lab coat and, if the participant showed concern for the learner and asked to stop the experiment, they would simply state set phrases such as "the experiment requires that you continue" or "I am responsible for what happens to the learner". The voltage could be increased gradually to a lethal level, and at a certain point the learners would protest and ask to leave the experiment, or would stop responding to questioning and appear completely unresponsive. What the participants did not know was that the learners were stooges working for Milgram and did not come to any harm at all.

The laboratory set-up for Milgram's Study of Obedience

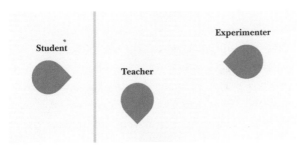

Milgram and his colleagues did not think that any, or many, of the participants would actually reach the point where they could cause harm to the learner, but what they found shocked the psychological community: 65 per cent of participants followed their instructions to the full, lethal voltage. As far as they knew, they had potentially killed the learner.

It seemed that an authority figure could indeed influence a person to commit horrendous acts, simply by stating their authority and suggesting that they would take ultimate responsibility for what took place. Milgram theorized that participants had switched from being in an autonomous state, when they felt that they were responsible for their own actions, to an agentic state, where they were acting as an "agent" for another person and therefore did not need to accept responsibility.

Milgram's study faced some criticism. It was argued that his sample of volunteers may have been more likely to follow orders simply because they were the kind of people to volunteer for a study like this, or that participants may have realized that the shocks were not real. But regardless of these criticisms, Milgram's study shocked the psychological community and his findings have been replicated in a variety of different cultures and conditions since.

Milgram's research represented a turning point in our understanding of social psychology and, as his biographer Thomas Blass stated, "It is not the kind of person we are that determines how we act, but rather the kind of situation we find ourselves in."

American psychologist **Philip Zimbardo** (1933–) went on to examine the effect that a very specific environment has on a person – that of a prison. In 1971 he conducted his now famous "Stanford Prison Experiment", which was funded by the US Office of Naval Research in an effort to study antisocial behaviour. He wanted to see if people's behaviour was altered when they were given a specific social role that carried with it a set of expected behaviours as well as a certain amount of anonymity.

In the study, 24 healthy, male, American college students volunteered to take part in a two-week prison simulation. They were assessed to ensure that they were psychologically and physically healthy, and that they did not already have a criminal background. They were then randomly assigned their roles, with half being assigned the role of prison guard and the other half being assigned the role of prisoner. In each group, nine of the participants took part while three were kept in reserve.

The guards attended a training session the day before the study began where they were told that they would work in daily shifts of eight hours, with three guards present at any given time. They were told not to harm the prisoners or withhold food and drink. They were, however, instructed to make sure that the prisoners were bored, fearful, lacked any privacy and understood that their lives during the study were entirely controlled by those in authority. In his book, *The Lucifer Effect*, Zimbardo explains that he told the guards: "We have total power in the situation. They have none." He wanted to remove the prisoners' understanding of their individual identity and make them feel powerless.

He ensured that both groups, prisoners and guards, felt removed from their individual identities by providing them with uniforms. The guards had khaki guard uniforms, batons and mirrored sunglasses. The prisoners wore orange smocks, slippers and a chain around one ankle. The prisoners even had their names taken from them and were instead referred to by numbers that were sewn into their uniforms.

When it was time for the study to begin the prisoners were arrested at their own homes. Zimbardo wanted his study to feel as real as possible for the participants, so officers from the local Palo Alto police department arrested each "prisoner" and subjected them to the usual booking procedures, including finger printing and strip searching, before they were taken to Zimbardo's mock prison environment and began their experience.

If you're thinking that it sounds as if Zimbardo had cooked up a recipe for disaster, you'd be right. After only a few hours some guards began to assert their authority, blowing whistles at 2.30 a.m. to wake the prisoners and force them to line up for what turned out to be the first of many counts. Prisoners were made to do press-ups as punishments and given mundane tasks to complete. On the morning of the second day, a group of prisoners began to revolt, barricading themselves in their cells. In response, the guards blasted the cells with fire extinguishers, broke into the cells, stripped the prisoners and removed their beds. They began to remove some of the rights that had been afforded to the prisoners and, instead, to use them as privileges, rewarding those prisoners who had taken a less active role in the rebellion.

These measures were taken in an effort to break the solidarity of the prisoners, and it worked. As the guards became more dominant and assertive, the prisoners became more submissive. After only six days, the study, which had been planned to last for two weeks, had to be called off. Several prisoners showed symptoms similar to those of a mental breakdown and it was feared that their mental and physical health was at risk.

Why the guards acted this way is a source of controversy. Zimbardo argued that they were conforming to the social role given to them, and had experienced "deindividuation", a term coined by American social psychologist Leon Festinger, in the 1950s, to describe a state where an individual person cannot be separated or recognized in a group. This means that a person is no longer acting as an individual, but is an anonymous member of a crowd, losing their individual morals and responsibilities. Social psychologists such as Zimbardo believed that this could lead to antisocial behaviour, such as rioting, looting and other aggressive behaviour, because people no longer felt a personal responsibility for what they were doing. The factors that can lead to deindividuation are arousal (emotional excitement), anonymity (becoming "lost" in the group) and diffused responsibility (everyone else is doing it...), all of which were experienced by the guards during the study.

However, critics of the study claim that Zimbardo created a situation that was bound to prove his theories right. Some believe that the young men were all acting their parts, and that any changes in the characteristics of the participants were down to youthful high jinks. The study took place in 1971, when reports of prison riots and police brutality had been in the news often, so it could be argued that the young men were simply acting out the stereotypical view of prison life at the time. By directly instructing the guards to ensure that the prisoners had no privacy or power, Zimbardo was artificially creating the situation he sought to observe. Some "guards" openly said that they felt that their behaviour was helping the experimenters. This is a phenomenon known as "demand characteristics", where a participant will alter their behaviour to meet the demands of the study in which they are taking part. Then, when Zimbardo did not intervene after the first few instances of the guards overstepping their boundaries, his silence was providing tacit consent for them to continue. Despite Zimbardo admitting in *The Lucifer Effect* that his "findings came at the expense of human suffering", and that he was sorry for not providing adequate oversight during the procedures, in 1973 the American Psychological Association (APA) conducted an ethics evaluation and concluded that all existing ethical guidelines had been followed.

After learning about this research it is perfectly natural to wonder what you would do if you were put in the same situation. We like to think that we act based on our own moral and ethical principles, but, as we have seen, our behaviour is not as simple as that. Theories regarding conformity, obedience and deindividuation can go some way towards explaining outrageous acts conducted by groups of people. Violent rioting, looting and the abuse of prisoners in complexes such as Abu Ghraib may seem less mysterious once we learn that we are so easily influenced by others. As disturbing as it may be to learn that our perceived autonomy is so easily influenced and manipulated by others, we can take comfort in the fact that we now have the knowledge to avoid "groupthink", to question the influence of authority and to take steps to avoid being manipulated.

The Humanistic Approach

The approaches we have discussed so far tend to take a deterministic view of human behaviour. They try to find specific, predetermined causes for behaviours (whether biological factors or experiences) that are often out of the control of the individual person. They also take what is known as a "nomothetic" approach when they study our psychology, which means that they attempt to explain human behaviour using a set of universal rules that apply to all people, for example this neurotransmitter will cause people to behave in a certain way, being fixated at the oral stage of development will cause a person to be a needy adult and so on. This is an unsettling view of human behaviour for many people, as it suggests that we actually have very little free will or control over our behaviour. It also raises important questions about how accountable we are for our actions, whether we are to blame for our crimes and whether or not we have the right to be proud of our achievements.

The humanistic approach rebels against these ideas and argues that each person is a unique individual, with a subjective experience of life and free will over their choices and behaviour. Using a humanistic perspective we can take personal responsibility for our actions and gain a sense of self-worth and purpose, which is very appealing after learning how easy some psychologists think it may be to predict and manipulate our behaviour! It is no coincidence that the first works linked to this approach were published in the 1940s, not long after B. F. Skinner first published his descriptions of operant conditioning in 1936 (see page 54), especially as Skinner later went on to argue that free will is an illusion. Humanistic psychology was a rebellion against the psychodynamic and behavioural approaches and their hijacking of our personal autonomy.

American psychologist **Abraham Maslow** (1908–1970), who went on to become president of the American Psychological Association, is commonly credited with sparking the humanistic approach with the publication of his "hierarchy of needs" theory in 1943. At the time, psychologists had mainly been concerned with explaining abnormal psychology and "fixing" psychological problems. Few had been concerned with the more philosophical questions about the human experience, such as feelings of purpose, achievement or growth.

Maslow's theory has been developed extensively since then, but essentially it suggests that humans are motivated to achieve certain basic needs, and only once these needs are met can we progress to a point where we can focus our attention on personal growth and self-actualization. At the bottom of Maslow's hierarchy are our basic physiological needs: food, water, sleep. Once these are satisfied we are able to fully access and attend to our "security" needs such as employment, resources and health. After that we can "level up" to meaningful relationships with friends and family, and to achieve and fully appreciate a sense of connection. A person who has achieved all of these things has status and recognition, their self-esteem is high and they have a sense of freedom regarding the choices they have in life. If all goes well, a small number of people may become self-actualized, and possibly experience a "peak moment" – a euphoric mental state where any sense of time and doubt is lost, minds are flexible and open to new, creative ideas and the world appears effortless. And who wouldn't want that?

IF THE ONLY TOOL YOU
HAVE IS A HAMMER,
YOU TEND TO SEE EVERY
PROBLEM AS A NAIL.

ABRAHAM MASLOW

Reflections on Maslow's hierarchy of needs

Maslow argued that some needs take precedence over others: for example basic physiological needs must be met before we can focus our attention on the next highest need. Do you agree with the order of these levels? Can you think of examples where someone has achieved some of the stages without the "base" needs below it? Do you think this is the same in every culture?

Self-actualization
desire to become the most that one can be

Esteem
respect, self-esteem, status, recognition, strength, freedom

Love and belonging
friendship, intimacy, family, sense of connection

Safety needs
personal security, employment, resources, health, property

Physiological needs
air, water, food, shelter, sleep, clothing, reproduction

Maslow's approach appealed to another American psychologist and fellow future president of the APA, **Carl Rogers** (1902–1987), who went on to develop this work further. His approach applied to so many areas of human psychology that he wrote 16 books and many journal articles in order to refine his theories, but we'll try our best to summarize the main points here.

Rogers believed that we are the true experts of our own psychology, and only we, as individuals, can reflect upon and explain our own behaviour and motivations. He emphasized how important our own point of view is, and argued that, in a way, the reality of a situation does not matter – it's how we perceive it. Therefore, in order to reach our full potential and achieve "self-actualization", there needs to be balance between three major personal perceptions: our self-worth, our self-image and our ideal self. All three of these factors must overlap and be in harmony, or be "congruent" with one another, if we are to reach our full potential. If they differ from one another, most especially if our self-image is very much different from our ideal self, then we are in a state of incongruence and our achievements (or at least our perception of them) are limited. Achieving congruence is the ideal.

However, it is very difficult for an incongruent person to achieve congruence on their own. Accurately reflecting on your own perceptions and motivations is challenging when they originated in your own mind and are already a result of your own reasoning, which is why Rogers advocated a very specific type of intervention known as "person-centred therapy". As the name suggests, this method of therapy is guided by the individual themselves and does not work on the assumption that the therapist is an all-knowing authority figure who is there to diagnose and "fix" your mental health. The therapist should listen but not judge, while the individual takes an active role in their therapy and is guided through a journey of self-discovery that is facilitated, but not controlled, by the therapist.

Rogers developed this therapeutic technique over several years, starting with a description of non-directive therapy in his 1942 publication, *Counseling and Psychotherapy: Newer Concepts in Practice.* This was in direct contrast to techniques used in "talking therapies" at the time, in which the therapist guided the sessions and provided possible answers or diagnoses. His work on client-centred therapy was published in 1951, and while the terms "non-directive" and "client-centred" may not appear to be conceptually very different, Rogers was taking steps to move away from defining the therapist–client relationship from the point of view of the therapist. Instead of using the term "non-directive" to describe what the therapist *should not* do, he was instead focusing on what the client *should* do, or be enabled to do. This phrasing was eventually replaced with the term "person-centred", but retains many of the original concepts.

While the humanistic approach can rightly be criticized for being subjective, with no way to truly measure concepts such as self-worth or actualization, its impact on talking therapies cannot be overstated.

Controversies in Psychology

In studying the complex and often subjective phenomena of the human experience, psychologists run the risk of reducing an intricate subject down to a simple set of rules and codes. Their theories and findings may imply that your behaviour is out of your control, and that it is predetermined by biological factors or experiences in your past. Furthermore, in order to conduct psychological research, it is sometimes necessary to manipulate and deceive those taking part in the research. Findings may reveal facts about human nature that we find uncomfortable to admit, and can have consequences beyond those intended or imagined by the psychologists behind them.

In the following pages, we will address the subject of ethics in psychological research, the interplay between subjective and scientific research methods, the benefits and drawbacks of a reductionist approach to behaviour and how determinism can impact our perception of free will.

THERE IS ROOM ENOUGH FOR
AN AWFUL LOT OF PEOPLE
TO BE RIGHT ABOUT THINGS
AND STILL NOT AGREE.

KURT VONNEGUT

ETHICS

In the previous chapters in this book we have seen that some studies had questionable ethics. For instance, we have discussed how Milgram led participants to believe, albeit briefly, that they had killed another human being, and Pavlov measured the saliva produced by dogs by surgically implanting saliva-catching vials into their muzzles as well as using electric shocks.

Fortunately, psychological research is now regulated by thorough guidelines designed to protect participants, both human and non-human. In the UK, ethical guidelines in psychology are advised by the British Psychological Society (BPS); and similar organizations exist in other countries. Such guidelines are in place to protect participants from both physical and psychological harm, and are based around four key principles:

1. Respect
2. Competence

3. Responsibility

4. Integrity

The first principle concerns **respect** for all persons. Psychologists must ensure that every participant in their research has been given enough detail regarding the procedures of the study to provide informed consent. This means that they understand what will happen to them during the study, and that they understand that they have the right to withdraw from the study at any time. A psychologist will usually produce a set of forms for participants to sign, which outline what the study is about and what the method will involve. The procedures should ensure that all participants' data and results are confidential, even if they are conducting a case study of a single person. At the end of the experiment the participants will also be given a full debrief, which should re-clarify the aims of the study and also explain that the participant has the right to withdraw their data if they wish to do so before the study is published.

Sometimes research designs might involve deception. For example, a psychologist could ask someone to take part in a memory test, but actually be intending to measure how they interact with other people in the room. Or they could ask a participant to read a book and talk about what they have learned, but the psychologist is actually observing their posture and mannerisms. If this is the case, then the full nature of the study must be explained clearly in the debrief. While deception is sometimes necessary in psychological research, it should never cause psychological harm or distress to someone taking part.

The second principle concerns the **competence** of those conducting the study. Psychologists are expected to maintain high standards in their work, and are expected to support each other in upholding this principle.

The third principle demands that psychologists **act responsibly**. Psychologists must protect participants from psychological and physical harm, and must also ensure that their research is socially and morally ethical.

The fourth principle emphasizes the need for **integrity** in the study of psychology. As well as having a responsibility to protect their participants, psychologists have a responsibility to the general public and to the wider scientific community. They should ensure that they publish true and accurate data and share their research through publication. They should evaluate their research and make any potential limitations of their methodology very clear so that others can accurately build on their research in the future. If a psychologist has any concerns over the practice of a colleague, they should raise this with the relevant professional body.

DON'T BECOME A MERE RECORDER OF FACTS, BUT TRY TO PENETRATE THE MYSTERY OF THEIR ORIGIN.

IVAN PAVLOV

PSYCHOLOGY AS A SCIENCE

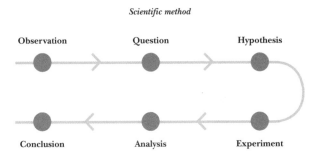

Scientific method

As you will have noticed throughout this book, the approaches taken to the study of psychology are broad and varied. They range from subjective and introspective subjects such as the nature of happiness, to subjects that are more commonly associated with "pure" sciences, such as the functioning of neurons or the physical structure of the brain.

Some areas of psychology, such as the psychodynamic approach, have been accused of being too subjective and unfalsifiable – too "unscientific" to be taken seriously. If a theory is falsifiable, that means that we can construct studies in order to test the theory and attempt to prove it wrong. In the psychodynamic approach for example, there is no way to "test" whether or not a person has experienced the Oedipus complex as Freud would have argued that the experience was repressed into their unconscious mind. It cannot be measured, so it cannot be falsified.

But that is not to say that these theories are unimportant. The psychodynamic approach has inspired generations of psychologists and many effective therapies. And, with the advent of new brain imaging techniques, some of Freud's seemingly unfalsifiable theories do in fact have some scientific backing. For example, studying the brains of sleeping participants reveals that the areas of the brain associated with conscious thought (the Ego) are dormant when we sleep, while the areas associated with basic biological instincts (the Id) are more active. This is in accord with Freud's theory that dreams are the result of unconscious urges crossing into the conscious mind while the Ego is at rest.

However varied the psychological approaches appear in their focus and research methodologies, psychologists ultimately strive to study human behaviour in a systematic and objective way. If psychologists wish to study the human mind and brain, it is by building on the work of the people before them: people who invented the microscope, who isolated a single neuron, who recognized there were electrical impulses running through those neurons. For their work to be built upon, psychologists must ensure that it is objective and replicable (others should be able to repeat your experiment to see if they find similar results). It must use the scientific method.

Compared to the older sciences, such as physics and chemistry, this is trickier for psychology. Psychologists are studying something that they often cannot see but that is affected by hundreds of variables, many of which are out of their control or that they may never have even considered could influence their results.

For example, if we were to make the bold claim that people who like dogs are better at baking cakes, we would have to make sure that all of our participants' results could be compared, by narrowing down exactly which type of cake we would like them to bake. We would then create a scale on which to judge their baking (a standardised one that could be applied reliably every time by whoever needed it, which would render the judges of *The Great British Bake Off* obsolete). We would also have to create a measurement in order to rate the participants' "liking" of dogs. After collecting our results, we would then have to use inferential statistics to decide if our findings could have just occurred by chance or whether they are the result of the variables we manipulated (i.e. are the results significant?). We would have to evaluate whether our findings would still be true if we tried to make our claim outside the tiny environment in which we carried out our study. Finally, further studies would be needed to identify possible reasons for our findings. We may have found a correlation, but that does not suggest that liking dogs causes an improvement in a person's baking skills. Psychologists must be incredibly knowledgeable about scientific research design to make any sort of reliable progress in explaining complex human behaviour. Most importantly, after research is complete psychologists then need to consider the impact of their results. Their research should undergo a peer review process before being published and they are expected to offer recommendations for future research and indicate who might find their results useful.

Psychology has gone through "phases", in the same way all fields of research do, but often psychologists are expanding on, or reacting to, the work of their predecessors. Even if it is only to act as a catalyst for a new approach, each branch of psychology, with their varied approaches to the study of the mind, can be seen to complement, influence and inspire another.

REDUCTIONISM VERSUS HOLISM

In order to study human behaviour it is usually necessary for a psychologist to focus on one particular variable at a time. They must reduce a very complex subject, for example depression, memory, aggression and so on, down to a few simple factors in order to be able to measure them. This is known as a reductionist approach and is based on the scientific principle of parsimony, meaning that complex phenomena should be explained using the simplest explanation possible.

Psychologists will identify a behaviour or phenomenon they would like to investigate, then design research that attempts to find correlations or cause-and-effect relationships with other factors. For example, Bandura wanted to measure the effect that witnessing violence had on children's behaviour. Loftus and Palmer wondered if the wording of a question could alter a person's memory of an event. Freud wondered if childhood experiences influence our behaviour as adults.

Focusing on one factor at a time is a necessary condition of trying to study human behaviour scientifically. However, this can lead to a rather simplistic view of human behaviour that excludes other possible factors. It can lose sight of the richness of human experience and the complexity of the interaction between our biology and our environment.

Examples of a reductionist approach in psychology:

- **Biopsychology**: Depression is caused by an imbalance of the neurotransmitter serotonin, and can be treated using drugs such as selective serotonin reuptake inhibitors.

- **Behaviourism**: Behaviour is a learned response to a stimulus, and can be explained by examining simple environmental factors.
- **Cognitive psychology**: The human mind acts like a computer, with input from the environment, internal mental processes and behavioural output.

Holism is an attempt to consider multiple factors when studying a behaviour. This approach considers the whole to be greater than the sum of its parts, and therefore the entirety of the human experience should be considered (or at least as much of it as possible) if we are to understand the true causes of behaviour. It is more difficult to objectively study cause and effect using this approach, which often relies on case studies to gain a deeper understanding of the multiple factors that influence a person's behaviour. However, this can mean that a much more in-depth analysis of a behaviour is possible and new avenues of investigation can be identified and, subsequently, investigated further in a reductionist way.

Examples of holistic approaches in psychology:

- **Psychoanalysis**: In-depth case studies considering multiple factors are often used in psychoanalytic research. Freud often conducted case studies of his patients to inform his theories. However, his theories were ultimately reductionist. For example, the simplification of the human psyche into the Id, Ego and Superego.

- **Humanism**: A true holistic approach to psychology, focusing on the self and a person's own perception of the self.

DETERMINISM VERSUS FREE WILL

Determinism is a difficult concept for many people to accept. We believe that we have free will and a free choice regarding our actions, reactions and decisions, but this is in conflict with some aspects of psychological research. Most approaches in psychology rely on a deterministic approach – an ability to determine the cause of a given behaviour – in order to explain the behaviour in question and treat it if necessary. For example, a strongly deterministic biological psychologist would suggest that your behaviour was genetically predetermined at birth by your genes, or a cognitive psychologist may argue that your behaviour is a response to a previously learned schema. In fact, this very defence has been used in court and can set a dangerous precedent in terms of how far we can be expected to take responsibility for our own actions.

However disturbing (or reassuring, depending on your perspective) a deterministic argument for our behaviour is, it is necessary in order for us to study human behaviour. In order to study the causes of behaviour, psychologists must often begin by assuming that there is an ultimate cause – that our behaviours have been caused by a biological mechanism or a previous experience, for example. As unsettling as it may be, it is a necessity if we are to study psychology scientifically.

The term "soft determinism" is used to describe an attempt to reconcile the human need to feel a sense of agency and control over our thoughts and behaviour, and the scientific need to develop laws in order to predict human behaviour. A soft deterministic approach would suggest that there are biological and environmental mechanisms that underlie our behaviour, but that, ultimately, we still have a choice regarding the impact they have on our thoughts and actions.

DON'T WORRY WHEN YOU ARE NOT RECOGNIZED BUT STRIVE TO BE WORTHY OF RECOGNITION.

ABRAHAM MASLOW

Conclusion

By this stage of the book, you have probably come to the conclusion that there is no single explanation for human behaviour, but you do now have a grounding in some of the best explanations we have so far. Our minds are fascinating, complex and, simultaneously, both measurable and immeasurable. There are some psychological assumptions that we can be pretty certain about, like the fact that certain areas of the brain are associated with certain behaviours, whereas other psychological assumptions are more subjective and require greater leaps of judgement, such as the impact of our unconscious mind.

We have also seen that the subjects studied by psychologists vary hugely, and this opportunity to study so many different areas of human (and animal) behaviour may be why psychology is one of the most popular subjects studied at UK universities (social sciences were the sixth most popular degree course in 2019).

Psychology is a dynamic field that is constantly evolving. If psychology aims to understand how people behave in the real world, and the real world is constantly changing, then being a psychologist demands that the successes of the past are built upon, while also creatively embracing new technologies. New fields of study are constantly growing and emerging like branches from the historical approaches, shaped by the fluidity of culture and society.

As daunting as it may seem to summarize a broad subject like psychology in a little book such as this, it is perhaps even more intimidating to predict the future of psychological research. As the world and our place in it change, the human race will also change and adapt, and there will be new challenges for psychologists to understand, explain and offer guidance for. You now have the tools and knowledge to embrace these new advances and see where the rivers of discovery are flowing.